Weblogs & New Media:
Marketing in Crisis

Weblogs & New Media: Marketing in Crisis

Charles Hugh Smith

2008

Trewe Press
Berkeley, California

Trewe Press
P.O. Box 4727
Berkeley CA 94704

Visit www.booksurge.com to order additional copies.

Weblogs & New Media:
Marketing in Crisis

Section One

"Marketing In Crisis" Is Both Critique And Guide.

1. "Standard Marketing" is in crisis, as it is maladapted to the global era of extended turmoil we are entering.

2. This book is a primer on how to build new, enduring ties to customers and stakeholders in the coming era of crisis by leveraging the largely misunderstood power of weblogs and New Media—what I call "The Power Yet to Come (TM)."

For better or for worse—and we all have some choice as to which of the two we will experience—the world is entering an extended era of disruption caused by the intersection of four mutually reinforcing long-term cycles, as illustrated on the cover diagram:

1. Peak oil, or the depletion cycle/end-game of the global economy's complete dependence on inexpensive, readily available petroleum/fossil fuels. (Green line)
2. The cycle of credit expansion and contraction (approximately 60-70 years), which is now beginning the transition from unsustainable credit expansion (bubble) to renunciation of debt (credit collapse) and global depression. (Blue line)
3. The generational cycle (4 generations or approximately 80 years) of American history that leads to nation-changing social,

political and economic upheaval. (The American Revolution: 1781 +80 years = Civil War, 1861 +80 years = 1941, World War II + 80 years = 2021.) (Purple line)

4. The 100+ year cycle of price inflation and stagnation of wages' purchasing power which began around 1901 is now reaching the final stage of widespread turmoil, shortages, famine, war, conflict and crisis. (Red line)

Within any complex system — and human culture and the global economy are certainly both complex systems — there are leverage points of varying strength.

The key leverage points that are easiest to change are:
1. Add an information feedback loop
2. Change a goal
3. The most powerful leverage point, and the one most culturally and institutionally resistant to change, is a paradigm or worldview (*Weltanschauung*).

As that is the most powerful leverage point, it is the one I am pursuing here.

A Note on Method and Language

As is already abundantly clear, I do not come from a marketing background or worldview, though as an entrepreneur I have marketed my ideas, my services and myself for decades. As an entrepreneur, I am well aware of the First Principle of capitalism, which is creative destruction. No firm or institution is too big to fail, and many become too unwieldy to survive a rapidly evolving world or paradigm. Small firms are not guaranteed survival, either; every market and provider will have to adapt successfully or face destruction.

Since I have been a student of powerful ideas for 40 years — a notion both obscured and described by the word philosophy — I naturally turn to ideas and cycles which have withstood the test of time and which retain predictive or explanatory powers beyond "trends du jour."

Most advertising and marketing are similar, much as automobiles have become very similar in shape, design and features. The reason is that they are all drawn from the same well of ideas, worldview and context/training.

I draw upon a different well. Having confessed my weakness for philosophy, proceed at your own risk.

These ideas are drawn both from history/philosophy and from my own experience in building a fast-growing and steadily expanding audience for my weblog, and from my study of marketing, weblogs and New Media. Expertise in these fields flows from Emerson's phrase: "Do the thing and you will have the power." That is, the experts are the ones who have taken their weblog/New Media audiences from near-zero to the hundreds of thousands/millions and who have created new bonds of loyalty with customers/stakeholders. I have attempted to distill the concepts common to enduringly successful (i.e. not a supernova which burns brightly for a moment and then recedes to a dark husk) New Media sites.

The following list of characteristics is not exhaustive; the field is too new and dynamic for anyone to claim a definitive understanding or account. I believe an understanding of these ideas and characteristics will help anyone whose financial survival depends on a business or organization's successful transformation in the era ahead.

Those with no stake will still gain from the intellectual exercise of disputing/contesting every concept and critique.

The four reinforcing trends will unleash unprecedented creative destruction.

Together, they form a bottleneck through which many firms, institutions and organizations will fail to pass.

The process of Creative Destruction is the essential fact about capitalism. Every business strategy acquires its true significance only against the background of that process and within the situation created by it.

Joseph Schumpeter

The Standard Model of advertising and marketing will produce fewer and fewer results as it fails to map the profound demographic, energy, cultural, technological and financial cycles which will dominate life and business for decades to come.

But in capitalist reality as distinguished from its textbook picture, it is not that kind of (price) competition which counts but the competition from the new commodity, the new technology, the new source of supply, the new type of organization—competition which commands a decisive cost or quality advantage and which strikes not at the margins of the profits and the outputs of the existing firms but at their foundations and their very lives.

The Web is widely understood to be that competitive advantage, but the nature of its marketing and relationship-building advantages have been masked by outdated paradigms of structure, advertising, marketing and CRM (customer relationship management).

Weblogs and New Media are perceived as part of that competitive advantage, but without a conceptual understanding, their advantages are lost in the slapdash miasma of websites, wikis, and other web technologies that constitute "Internet strategies" for most firms/organizations. Understanding and implementing those advantages is the heart of "The Power Yet To Come" (TM).

The wrenching demographic, financial and cultural changes which will dominate the decades ahead have long been visible to those with a grasp of history, but they are just now entering public awareness. Every firm's prosperity—and eventually, its survival—depends on adapting forcefully and insightfully to these profoundly disruptive global cycles.

Competitive Advantage Begins with Insight

"Solutions" are predetermined by how the "problem" is framed. If the "problem" is improperly framed, the "solution" will lead us away from addressing the actual problem. Problems cannot always be "solved" with the same level of thinking that framed them.

Identifying competitive advantages in a hyper-competitive world which is entering an extended era of turmoil must begin with an understanding of the operant contexts of our time and the two models of history which illuminate them.

History can either be viewed as proceeding along an innate vector (entelechy) toward a goal (*telos*) or as a cyclical process which "echoes" previous cycles.

There is abundant, irrefutable evidence that the global economy is facing an unprecedented confluence of crises/challenges which will threaten the survival of institutions, corporations and organizations. "Business as usual" will doom those clinging to the status quo to the ash-heap of history.

Ideas are not trends, and trends are not entelechies.

The idea which offers the best account/map of an era's causal conditions will endure until a new paradigm/account takes root which offers a more insightful, more accurately predictive worldview/mapping. An enduring idea *totalizes* history and current experience, making sense of events and causes which previous ideas/models did not adequately describe or explicate.

A trend is either an ephemeral cultural fad or a statistical construct; as the causal factors lie elsewhere, a trend's predictive value is limited to statistical probabilities. But probability is not causation, and the entelechies which are unfolding are causal; thus, predicting behavior based on recent trends is a superficial exercise.

Unlike a trend, an entelechy generates its own future from within itself; the seeds of its future course (or end-state, goal, *telos*) are already implicit in its seed/initial state. For example, the discovery of oil already contained its future depletion; the end-state and path was defined by petroleum's nature and its discovery in an industrializing era and nation, not by statistical probabilities or trends-du-jour.

Marketing software that seeks to predict consumers' future purchases or interests from data-mining/algorithmic extrapolations of past purchases is thus a statistical exercise in trend-seeking. Without an idea that accounts for the consumer's future behavior—an idea which maps the inner logic of the consumers' priorities and the worldview which shaped them—or an entelechy that dominates the era's worldview, the statistical/software construct is fundamentally powerless as a causal guide.

Statistically, there is a slim chance that you might strike oil in your backyard. But geologically, there is no causal evidence that oil could have formed there by any known processes. Thus it is not just statistical bad luck no major oil fields have been found since the early 1970s; geologically, all the possible areas which possess the specific conditions for the accumulation of oil have been explored.

Thus there may well be a statistical basis to believe in huge future oil finds, and the trend toward higher proven reserves may suggest ever-larger discoveries of oil lie ahead, but the causal factors of geology, chemistry and locale (the petroleum entelechy) are traveling down a vector with only one end-state: depletion.

Worldview and Context

The German word *Weltanschauung* denotes both worldview and context. When a new worldview takes root, the "dominant paradigm" shifts. Understanding the operant *Weltanschauung* is the first essential step to gaining insight into competitive advantage. The operant contexts of the era ahead are:

- Increasing global competition for physically limited/constrained FEW resources (food, energy, water) and unpredictable, highly disruptive shortages.
- Decreasing discretionary income and financial resources, increasingly burdensome debt loads, tax burdens and FEW costs.
- Overabundance of manufactured goods and marketing.
- Small fluctuations in supply chains due to bottlenecks/local shortages exert increasingly outsized effects on global markets (the Pareto 4/64 rule, a.k.a. "the 80/20 rule.").
- Global aging places unprecedented, unaffordable entitlement demands on governments, communities and families in both developed and developing nations.
- Post-colonial conflicts, ethnic /tribal strife and geopolitical jockeying for resources continue to splinter post-Cold War stability, while widening income and asset inequalities fuel globalization's discontents.
- Environmental degradation of water and air quality

limit global production of agricultural/"renewable" resources.

- The three major asset classes (stocks, bonds and real estate) are moving globally in unison; having reached overextended valuations in a 25-year cycle, they are now declining together in a cycle of roughly proportional duration.

- Employee (and hence family and community) security continues eroding as global wage arbitrage further fractures employers' ability and willingness to provide long-term security in employment and pension/medical care benefits. The new models are economywide independent contracting or a black-market economy operating beneath a shrinking elite defending their secure jobs against any reduction in entitlements.

- The creative destruction of distribution oligopolies (TV networks, et al.), previous forms of competitive advantage (offshoring, long supply chains, just-in-time inventories, etc.) and Standard Model marketing continues apace.

- Diminishing discretionary income across all revenue streams (consumers, business and governments) and a reversion to thrift from debt-fueled spending decreases the competitive advantages of "luxury" and "branding" and increases the competitive advantages of quality, loyalty and community.

The ultimate value of wealth in any form is energy.

Without energy, wealth in any form—precious metals, technology, ships, data—is reduced to either a capital trap or a stranded asset.

Previous high civilizations (ancient Greece, The Roman Empire, the Tang Dynasty in China, ancient India, the Incas, Mayans and Aztecs, the Mediterranean circa 1550, etc.) relied on human, animal and wind energy (sailing ships) to create agricultural surpluses which then enabled production of goods and global trade. (Rome, India and China were trading partners long before 1 AD.) Our current civilization relies almost entirely on cheap, abundant energy derived from rapidly depleting petroleum.

Energy is thus the first subject of any contextual analysis.

Some believe that energy resources follow a pattern which is essentially entelechal, that is, which proceeds along an innate vector of ever-higher energy densities: wood is replaced by whale oil which is replaced by coal which is replaced by petroleum which is replaced by nuclear, and so on.

Plentiful evidence suggests that this vector is not so straight or assured as many believe.

Hubbert's Peak describes with uncanny accuracy the depletion curveset of petroleum on any scale: one well, one nation, or the entire global petroleum complex.

Technical and scientific innovation tends to follow what might be termed a cyclical pattern in which long periods of relative stability, e.g. "normal science," are broken intermittently by paradigm shifts. In Natural Selection, this idea is embodied by the concept of Punctuated Equilibrium.

Periods of relative stability are characterized by a peculiar blindness to evidence of change. Thus we have projections which anticipate a magical abundance of fuels—an additional 125 billion gallons per year above today's consumption—even as the only large-scale, reliable source of high-energy-density fuel, petroleum, is declining rapidly.

(Global demand for petroleum fuels is expected to rise

from 275 billion gallons a year in 2005 to 400 billion gallons in 2030.)

In April 2008, Russia announced that 2008's production would not reach last year's total, nor would any future year match 2007's output. Similar media reports document Mexico's arrival on the downside of Hubbert's Peak.

In the sunny worldview of believers in technology and unlimited resources — a key tenet of this belief is that limitations are only chimera of the mind, not of the real world — the "next phase of ever-greater energy abundance" will be based on a mix of technologies and resources: next-generation breeder nuclear reactors, tar-sand extraction, seabed methane, tidal motion generation, solar, wind and geothermal power, gasification of coal, biofuels based on switchgrass and/or algae or sugarcane, and the clean technologies based on hydrogen fuel cells and electric vehicles.

While each of these technologies has promise, none scale-up to the levels of energy usage which current extrapolations project just a few years in the future.

The inaccuracy of long-term projections is reflected in various financial news reports, one of which (published in *Barrons*) predicted (as of early 2006) that crude oil would remain well below $100/barrel through 2010 and beyond.

Meanwhile, in the real world, oil already exceeded $135/barrel in May 2008. This then begs the question: could the seemingly astronomical sum of $300/barrel be reached not in distant 2020, but in the not-so-distant future of 2009 or 2010?

Given Hubbert's Peak and the reports of declining production, future sources of energy must not just add 125 billion gallons of fuel (of the same energy density as high-energy gasoline/jet fuel), they must also replace up to 75

**billion gallons of current petroleum-based fuels which will
be missing due to depletion by 2020.**

Which mix of these technologies can possibly provide
the equivalent energy of 200 billion gallons of gasoline, which
contains, by weight, approximately the same energy as dynamite?
According to the EIA's (Energy Information Administration)
2006 Global Energy Markets projections, the global demand
for energy is essentially insatiable, with demand expected to
rise from 450 quadrillion BTUs in 2006 to 722 quadrillion BTUs
in 2030, even as the source of 90% of the world's vehicular fuels,
petroleum, has already entered its decline/depletion stage. Even
coal has limitations on its usage, limits set by transportation
costs and by climate change (greenhouse gas release and sulfur-
dioxide, the cause of acid rain).

From an engineering perspective, as opposed to the
blissfully optimistic true believer in "limitless abundance," all
of these alternative sources of energy have severe limitations.
Until they can be demonstrated on a large scale at a cost
comparable to other sources, belief in their future is essentially
religious in nature.

Even if some do scale up, they will simply be replacing
energy lost to declining petroleum reserves. This is analogous
to the Red Queen's Race, in which the Queen is running simply
to stay in place.

Just as a brief, by no means exhaustive listing:

- There are only two breeder-reactors in existence, and
  the plutonium they produce poses a security risk.
  Uranium is also in a Hubbert's Peak-type decline,
  with 70 years' supply of ore remaining being the most
  optimistic estimate.
- Solar power requires either petroleum backup or

massive storage capacity which has yet to be proven on a large scale. Large-scale solar-generated electricity, located for efficiency in deserts, must be delivered to markets hundreds or thousands of miles away, with an energy loss of approximately 50% in the transmission.

- If the entire state of Iowa's agricultural production were devoted to biofuels, the ethanol/biodiesel produced would meet at best only 12% of the U.S. vehicular fuel demand.

- Algae-based biofuels are far more efficient than corn-based biofuels, but the many complexities of feedstock, distillation, etc. have yet to be solved on an industrial scale.

- Wind energy has the potential to supply a percentage of total U.S. energy consumption, but it requires on-demand backup for low-wind periods and/or large-scale storage technologies.

- Due to technical and physical constraints (moving entire mountains of tarry soil, the need for natural gas in quantity to heat the oil-sands, etc.), the oil-sands of Canada can only produce 2.5 million barrels of oil a day, even at full peak production—less than 15% of the oil the U.S. consumes every day.

Many of these inefficiencies can be improved over time, given sufficient investment and time, but while the U.S. will spend over $400 billion on imported oil in 2008, it collectively spends but a fraction of that sum on alternative fuel development.

Conservation via increasing mechanical and electrical efficiencies has been shown to provide the cheapest, fastest method of reducing demand without reducing output, but conservation currently has low political appeal and support.

In the absence of politically-imposed regulations/

restrictions, the "market" is supposed to address all FEW (food, energy, water) cost spikes. The problem with naive reliance on the marketplace is that FEW crises arise with fractal speed and unpredictability. If a large-scale drought occurs, new water sources and hundreds of miles of aqueducts cannot be built fast enough to resolve the crisis. For example, the California Water Management System is purportedly the largest public works project in the world and it required decades to construct.

If petroleum doubles in price from today's levels with the same alacrity that it rose from $60 to $120, even if auto makers begin manufacturing highly efficient vehicles, it will take an estimated 20 years to change over the entire U.S. fleet of some 230 million trucks and autos.

The faith that change/crisis will move leisurely enough to enable market reactions to successfully correct large-scale supply/demand imbalances is an artifact of a past rooted in an abundance of commodities and scalable manufacturing. This belief is no longer grounded by a fact-based worldview.

How do energy depletion and the other three cycles relate to the competitive advantages of weblogs and New Media?

Let's begin by referring back to creative destruction:

The process of Creative Destruction is the essential fact about capitalism. Every business strategy acquires its true significance only against the background of that process and within the situation created by it.

But in capitalist reality as distinguished from its textbook picture, it is not that kind of (price) competition which counts but the competition from the new commodity, the new technology, the new source of supply, the new type of organization—competition which commands a decisive cost or quality advantage and which strikes not at the margins of the profits and the outputs of the existing firms but at their foundations and their very lives. (Joseph Schumpeter)

The optimist's view that history is an entelechy following a vector toward higher energy density, higher consumption, longer lives, stable peace and increasing liberty is facing unprecedented challenges on fundamental physical, demographic and financial fronts.

This Hegelian view of history fired both the idealistic Marxist ideologies of the 19th and 20th centuries, and the progressive/liberal Western Civilization view that humankind was inevitably growing wealthier and wiser.

The alternative view—that history is essentially cyclical—is supported by geographical and financial data stretching back hundreds of years.

Rather than choose between the two views, we should consider the possibility that just as light is both wave and particle, perhaps history is both entelechal and cyclical. The challenges the world faces within the next few years/decades certainly seem to mix both teleological and cyclical forces/trends:

1. Skyrocketing energy costs will act as an enormous global tax on consumption.
As energy costs rise for transportation, fertilizers, materials, mined ore, food, and indeed every item currently mined, fabricated, grown, traded and shipped, consumers in every nation and every socioeconomic status will have significantly less wealth to spend on anything but life's essentials. The effects of reduced disposable/discretionary income on global businesses, NGOs, non-profits, and governmental agencies will be extraordinarily pervasive.
2. Just as FEW (food, energy, water) imbalances impose an increasingly burdensome and volatile tax on

global consumption, demographics which are already set in motion guarantee that huge Baby Boom generations in Europe, North America, China, Japan, India and elsewhere will be retiring/exiting the workforce just as their respective governments and employers find their revenues declining.

While denial has worked so far, the inability of governments to fund trillions of dollars in promised pensions and healthcare benefits is obvious to anyone who examines the demographic facts. This will also act as an additional global tax on wage earners, who must face supporting elderly parents and paying for their healthcare even as the human population ages on an unprecedented scale.

3. The Kondratieff Cycle suggests that the global asset bubbles which are just starting to deflate have a long way to go before the next cycle of financially healthy/stable growth can begin.

The Kondratieff Cycle captures the cyclical nature of debt accumulation through excessive borrowing, and the inevitability of debt repudiation as the end-state of that extreme leverage/euphoria, which is then renounced in a lengthy crash/depression that lays the foundation for a new cycle of productive growth.

What is truly unprecedented is that this low point (which typically corresponds to global depression) coincides with a global crisis in energy supply and a demographic time-bomb in which the retired/elderly are so numerous that there will soon be only two or three workers for every retiree in an era of double-digit growth in healthcare costs.

No asset class which has experienced a bubble—real estate, stocks, non-energy commodities and even bonds—will be spared from severe depreciation as assets are sold to fund retirements and as the global "glut of savings"/low-cost lending of surplus dollars dries up in a global consumer recession/depression.

Pensions both public and private which were once considered well-funded will be revealed as woefully underfunded and unable to pay out the benefits and pensions which were expected.

As capital pools and consumer spending both contract, government's ability to borrow or raise ever-larger sums from taxation will decline even as demands for promised entitlements increases sharply in both developed and developing nations.

4. Globally, public health will be under increasing stress from both persistent current trends (obesity, particulate air pollution, resistant bacteria, water-borne diseases, HIV, diseases of overconsumption, diseases of malnourishment, etc.) and disruptions, scarcities or outright shortages of food and water.

None of these pernicious trends show any sign of abatement, despite major efforts at amelioration. No crisis is necessary to push global public health over a tipping point; it will require only the momentum of current trends continuing unabated.

The hyper-growth of mega-cities/mega-slums with concentrations of 15-30 million residents in what are essentially islands of extreme resource consumption are creating densities which enable disease vectors to spread quickly through heretofore unimaginable numbers of people.

The concept of "tipping point" has many applications in such situations, not just in terms of public health but in terms of increasingly precarious supplies of FEW resources (food, energy, water) and the equally fragile export of waste (sewage, garbage, etc.) from sprawling, high-density mega-cities.

Perhaps even more useful is the Pareto Principle, which describes how the "critical few" (4%) exert outsized influence on the "trivial many" (64%). In cases of public health and supply of FEW assets, a 4% shift can trigger enormous effects. Recent shortages of grain illustrate the principle rather alarmingly.

Again, even as financial declines reduce governments' ability to borrow freely—the past borrowing of trillions will finally come back to haunt the many national governments which borrowed so freely in prosperous times—the demands of the public for more spending on healthcare will rise along with the median age of the populations worldwide.

5. "The End of History" which was welcomed just a decade ago has been replaced by a sober realization that deeply rooted post-colonial and ethnic/regional tensions were only suppressed, not resolved, by the Cold War.

The gleefully anticipated entelechy of triumphant liberty and free-market capitalism has been upended by older, darker entelechies of ethnic, tribal and geopolitical conflicts that were forced underground during the Cold War. Just as these ancient rivalries have been freed to resume their jockeying for influence and power, the world is facing permanent scarcity of FEW resources (food, energy, water) which will exacerbate these rivalries as well as add new ones.

6. The constant geographical shifting of manufacturing for increasingly slight competitive advantages and the deployment of industrial robots both augur an era of overabundance of manufactured goods and a sustained global surplus of labor.

Pricing power, already under pressure, will vanish for most non-FEW related goods, interrupted by brief spikes of marketing/technological advantages that vanish in ever-shorter cycles. The "low-hanging fruit" has long since been stripped and even the higher fruit is gone. New device features no longer offer competitive advantage for even one design cycle; the number and scope of existing features in manufactured goods ensure that each additional feature adds less and less value to the end user. The "trivial many" have little influence.

To reduce expenses and increase competitive flexibility, employers exposed to global competition have shed the model of long-term employment in favor of flexible contract labor. The only alternative to global labor insecurity is the highly regulated, high-taxation continental European model in which a relative elite gains government or government-mandated security while a lesser class of unlucky/less fortunate workers are relegated to a "black-market" underground cash economy with little or no security. This is also the operative model in Third World kleptocracies.

7. Extraordinarily brittle/fragile delivery systems dependent on long supply chains and bottlenecks will be vulnerable to unpredictable fractal breakdowns and disruptions. Incremental improvements no longer ameliorate the underlying supply/demand imbalances.

Spot shortages are already creating a feedback loop of fear-based hoarding which then exacerbates the perceived shortage into a real one. For example: if everyone in the U.S. tops off their vehicle fuel tank, that simple act multiplied by 230 million hoarding consumers will drain all gasoline reserves in a matter of days, creating the very shortage the consumers feared.

Inadequate investment in electrical systems and refinery infrastructure in the U.S. has further weakened the physical plant of the nation, creating additional vulnerabilities. In China, massively inefficient generation and delivery systems for electricity and water raise the likelihood of disruptions/shortages/public health crises in that nation. These same limitations and vulnerabilities are common to many nations.

Invoking the Pareto Principle once again, we can anticipate that even if only 4% of the population suffer from disruptions in water, food, electricity or petroleum supplies, the consequences may ripple through two-thirds of the entire population.

Incremental improvements that had an outsized effect in the beginning of any cycle—the Pareto Principle again—draw diminishing returns. The "low hanging fruit" is again a fitting analogy, as it captures the essential limits of incremental improvements. Examples of the principle abound: the first round of obvious efficiencies in a company, process or device reap much greater rewards than later iterations. The first injection of borrowed money quickly boosts production/revenue but later borrowing provides less and less leverage, and so on.

This is the illusion of incremental change.

Since the global supply chain and developed-world production systems have already reaped the easy, high-return efficiencies, attempts to overcome shortages in petroleum/energy/food/water with incremental improvements will fail to resolve the global imbalances. Resistance to dramatic political/lifestyle changes will be overcome only when all other incremental alternatives have been exhausted and crises can no longer be ignored.

While rising prices may be absorbed, sporadic shortages of essential commodities will lay bare the inadequacies of incremental "solutions."

8. Just as an overabundance of manufactured goods reduces prices and profits to zero, the overabundance of marketing and advertising effectively reduces the value of all standard marketing to near zero.
The predictable result is already in evidence: the consumer is increasingly inured to all marketing. The ability to ignore the clutter and distraction of advertising and marketing is

abundantly visible in rapidly declining click-through rates and the failure of most ad campaigns to create sales or mindshare in an era of declining discretionary income.

Also predictably, the response to this lower sensitivity has been to seek out whatever marginal virgin marketing territory remains unexploited: text messaging, the floors of supermarkets, videos on YouTube, ersatz "word of mouth" campaigns, etc.

The more ads and marketing there are, the less effect each has. This is the law of diminishing returns in full bloom.

This lower sensitivity to marketing coupled with lower disposable income—the first such sustained decline in 25 years—presages an extraordinarily difficult time for those tasked with generating new sales and keeping existing customer bases intact. As companies and organizations seek to survive global declines in disposable income and revenues, the poor leverage of expensive standard marketing campaigns will become increasingly obvious.

There is a generational context to this decline of sensitivity.

The Baby Boom generation was raised on simplistic but visually powerful advertising on the "new medium" of television; the Boomers have remained susceptible to mass-marketed (reductionist) imagery in ways that the next generation simply does not share. As Boomers retire and their income drops, the share of consumers who respond to standard mass-marketing techniques will decrease.

9. What constitutes status and prestige will undergo substantial transformations as scarcity of essential commodities collides with overabundance of manufactured goods and marketing.

Where in the past a mass-produced consumer good could (with sufficient slight-of-hand) be presented as status enhancing, global overabundance of virtually all mass-produced goods (both legitimate and pirated) has eroded the value of retail/consumption status. Luxury brands such as Mercedes and BMW have cheapened their appeal with lower-cost production lines which sport the coveted logo; other luxury brands have found the easy availability of perfect pirated copies has eroded the all-important associations of wealth and status.

In a world flooded with knock-offs and ever more strained attempts at prestige (the Gold card of the 80s became the Platinum Card of the 90s which begot the Diamond card of the 2000s, etc.), the next source of prestige and status will be that which cannot be mass-produced: experience.

Increasing scarcity, diminishing entitlements and the collapse of the debt-fueled asset bubbles will lead to a change in the *weltanschauung* of prestige; gaudy pretentiousness will be viewed as both dangerous (as it highlights growing disparities of wealth) and passe/gauche. The new prestige will be more private and experience-based, not consumption-based.

10. As supply/demand imbalances in FEW (food, energy, water) and the iron hand of demographics tightens its irreversible stranglehold on government's revenues and entitlement expenses, a global loss of faith in institutions will foster backlash/blowback and social disorder.

Expectations (i.e. our private inner maps of the future), lofted so high by the past 25 years of global expansion, cheap commodities and wealth creation via financial "innovations" (previously known as asset bubbles and debt), will be a powerfully destabilizing force globally.

It is a psychological truism that those with few expectations for betterment tend to persevere and be happy despite low status and income as they view themselves as sacrificing for the future benefit of the family and their children.

But those with high expectations for wealth, status, prestige, leisure and artistic expression find even modest disappointment a bitter gruel indeed. Thus the economic downturn in Hong Kong had little effect on the happiness of the city's many maids, but it exacted a devastating toll on their status/wealth-driven, high-expectation employers.

While many voices comment approvingly on the hundreds of millions of Asian citizens whose incomes have been raised dramatically by the global shift of manufacturing to China, Southeast Asia and India, few have commented on how those same citizens' expectations have been raised even higher. As the unrealistic expectations created by asset-bubbles and a cheerleading media are crushed by FEW shortages, global recession, a decline in asset valuations and borrowing power and a reduction in promised entitlements, the anger and frustration which will be released may find political voice.

Though it is largely glossed over in the ever-optimistic business media, globalization has not provided all participants the glowingly positive results trumpeted by various business books and well-paid think-tank pundits. While globalization has benefited those living in rule-of-law nations, to those living in kleptocracies/oligarchies then the mechanisms of globalization are legally obscure, politically abstract and largely hidden from media inquiry or regulatory investigation.

As the vulnerabilities and extreme fragility of globalization becomes manifest on the local and national levels, many populations will react against whatever forces they can identify as causes or enablers of their suffering/shortages, and globalization's minions (global corporations, etc.) will make plausible targets for their wrath.

11. Media decentralization and digital distribution will continue disrupting political hierarchies and once-secure media/channel oligopolies.

In the rush to exploit the new territories, marketers are finding their message has been severely diffused by the rapidly expanding universe of media outlets.

The old paradigm of reductionist, mass-distributed ads and marketing has been weakened to the point of obsolescence.

All paradigms are protected by the inertial mass of past investment: investments of capital, lives and belief systems made over decades. To say advertising simply doesn't work as it once did is to challenge the same comforting faith in technology and "progress" implicit in the belief that abundance can only increase.

12. The mass production/reductionist model of marketing is declining in efficacy.
Just as large schools and universities essentially applied the mass-production factory model of 20th century industry to education, so advertising/marketing applied the model to selling one-size-fits-all products via mass media (newspapers, magazines, then radio, television and now the Internet and its peer-to-peer/email/IM offspring).

The advances of "big science" in the 19th and 20th century were made by reducing a multitude of observations and data (effects) down to a handful of simple laws (causes) which were shown to explain the forces of Nature: gravity, thermodynamics, the Special Theory of Relativity, Quantum mechanics, etc.

In a similar fashion, mass marketing sought a single ad, slogan or image which could persuade millions of different consumers that they would extract uniquely individual benefits (that is, status) from acquiring a mass-produced brand-name good: one size fits all was matched by one ad motivates all. The slogan or image did not require a connection to the actual product; it needed only to spark a universal attraction to word play or introduce a myth-based image which plucked one of humankind's inner emotional strings.

As the global marketplace faces pressures and crises of unprecedented scope and reach, as organizations and consumers everywhere face new constraints on discretionary income, revenues and entitlements, the standard tools of marketing have worn out. Despite a proliferation of products and marketing channels, the paradigm remains rooted in mass production of consumables marketed via mass media broadcasting. A YouTube video is no more personal or targeted or active than a TV ad or an Internet banner ad; much of what has been heralded as New Media is essentially an extension of Old Media broadcasting. Standard Marketing applied to these simulacrum "New Media" remains passively reductionist in nature.

13. The population most susceptible to Standard Marketing is the very population that will soon have near-zero discretionary income. The classic hubris of marketing, and indeed of any business, is to assume that a rising tide which is raising all consumers' wealth and disposable income—and thus their susceptibility to marketing—results not from long-wave cycles of tides rising and falling but from the genius of a marketing campaign or product.

But a consumer with no discretionary income, savings or credit cannot be a buyer or customer, no matter how influenced he or she may be by a clever marketing campaign or cute advert.

The Pareto Principle suggests only a small percentage of the populace will have disposable income, savings or borrowing power—and it is this population who is most skeptical of advertising and most inured to Standard Marketing.
The people who watch 8 hours of television a day ("the trivial many") will have little money to spend on anything

other than energy, food and shelter—and perhaps prescription medications if the cost isn't too dear. The people who will control the vast majority of discretionary funds watch little TV or any other media, for they are too busy and under too much pressure to remain productive to be avid consumers of any media unrelated to their work.

Standard Marketing will thus fail to generate sales, customer loyalty or any other positive metric. With the survival of the firm or organization at stake, a new paradigm must be found that maps the new world created by these four intersecting long cycles:

1. Peak oil, the depletion cycle/end-game of petroleum/ fossil fuels.
2. The Kondratieff Cycle of credit expansion and contraction.
3. The four-generation cycle of American history.
4. The 100+ year cycle of price inflation and declines in wages' purchasing-power.

Section One Summary

Though it is comforting to assume the history of energy and economic development is entelechal, i.e. traveling along a predestined vector toward higher energy densities and consumption and greater distributed wealth for both the developed and developing nations, there is ample evidence that we are heading down a vector to depletion, widespread shortages, restricted supply and consumption, and growing income inequality. At the same time, history remains cyclical and the intersection of depletion with cyclical peaks in geopolitical instability and the cyclical nadir of financial stability are creating unprecedented challenges in demographics, energy, the environment, finance and geopolitics.

Secondary effects of the above trends will apply extreme pressures on every industry and service globally, including tourism/leisure, urban design, law enforcement, housing, transportation, government and agriculture, to name but a few.

Various entelechies which seemed to extend indefinitely just a decade ago—higher energy densities, benign demographic trends, financial leveraging of assets and asset-based derivatives, geopolitical stability, ever-rising resource extraction and increasing global wealth—are reversing or coming to an end.

Capitalism's chief mode of change—creative destruction—will rule the era with an unprecedented, relentless tenacity.

With Crisis Comes Opportunity

With crisis comes great opportunity, of course, and those with the right products at the right moment in time will undoubtedly find robust markets for water filters, alternative energy sources, high-mileage vehicles, new anti-bacteriological agents and so on.

Entelechal depletion will intersect with cyclical renaissance as new entelechies such as sustainable energy take hold. Those who understand the two forces are the most likely to find or fashion competitive advantage amidst the fractal crises and disruptions.

But every business without a painfully utilitarian crisis-alleviation product or service will face the extreme challenges of selling in a global recession that reduces discretionary spending of consumers, business and government alike as epochal feedback loops slash spending and increase competition.

Management will be challenged to strip away expenses fast enough to keep pace with falling revenues even as they must retain and remoralize productive employees, and strategists will have to grapple with the inconvenient fact that China-India and the rest of the Asian economies are no longer catapults to new sales and markets.

Long-standing entelechies which are drawing to a close include Standard Model Marketing, which will have to adapt to a cultural milieu dominated by scarcity, shortages, broken entitlement promises and a shift from debt-fueled carefree consumption and flamboyant excess to hoarding, thrift, quality and community.

As tempting as it is to assume this turning is merely cyclical—and undoubtedly there will be short-term cycles at work within these long-term cycles—there is also evidence that the methodologies which have guided advertising and marketing for decades are no longer persuading their desired audiences or reaching their sales goals. Incremental modifications in the Standard Model are drawing diminishing returns; gaining competitive advantage via mass marketing is becoming ever more elusive.

Like a gas-guzzling shiny vehicle getting 14 miles to the gallon as oil climbs to $150 per barrel, the Standard Model still works—but the returns are diminishing rapidly even as the costs are rising steeply.

In the vernacular: the bag of tricks has been exhausted/ depleted; the ads on every available surface, the bogus "word of mouth" subterfuges planted as "content" on weblogs, the gimmicks, the branding ads in high-gloss magazines, the clever television spots with lizards or turtles, the Web banner ads nobody clicks on anymore, the misguided contextual ads which offer unintended targets for consumers' mockery, the focus groups, the segmenting of "early adopters" and indeed, the entire Standard Model reductionism has, like cheap fossil fuel, run its course. Those who cling to obsolete models will suffer creative destruction.

With these contexts in mind, we turn now to an examination of the Standard Model and how weblogs and New Media offer a low-profile, low-cost but very powerful competitive advantage to those who understand the principles of "the power yet to come."

Section Two

One Ad Campaign No Longer Fits All: A Polemic On The Exhaustion Of The Broadcast/Propaganda Model

The Reductionist Model had a glorious run in the 20th century in a wide swath of endeavors, from medicine to fascism.

In medicine, microbial-caused diseases were conquered by "one drug cures all" antibiotics. In a vast array of consumer goods, manufacturing a single item with minor variations in giant factories lowered the cost of goods and enabled a consumer culture to spread from a monied elite to hundreds of millions of workers.

In marketing, myth-based imagery and sloganeering not only sold mass-produced goods, they also effectively sold entire populations on fascism. In appealing to humans' innate desire for prestige, self-worth, purpose and shared glory, both fascism and mass marketing shared the same toolbox.

The primary tool was broadcasting, starting with the print media and then reaching new levels of influence via radio and television and now the Internet.

With these tools in hand, marketers and politicians alike found they could shape their target audiences' *Politics of Experience*, providing simulacrums of authenticity and community via broadcasted slogans and imagery carefully crafted to satisfy deep-seated yearnings for self-worth, purpose, novelty and belonging. Actual living-in-the-world experience was replaced with highly stimulating, emotionally charged simulations which, once planted and nurtured via repetition, were then "experienced" as authentic.

The most infamous "brand" logo of the era, the Nazi swastika, painstakingly designed by Hitler himself, simply mirror-imaged the Buddhist "logo" revered in the East for millennia.

Mass marketing successfully exploited the human need for connection by offering a pathway to this need via essentially passive consumption. Action in the world was reduced to consumption, and any remaining active experience was harnessed to mass-produced consumer goods. In a simple analogy, the cardboard box of childhood play was replaced with "authentic" spaceships, cars, etc. which replaced imagination with a fad/ad-driven profitable consumable that would soon lose favor to the next definition of "cool."

As even the rudest peasant shack now contains a radio and television and wealthier consumers have run through every possible iteration of the mass-produced object, a devolution of ownership has taken hold. As objects are ever more speedily replaced and tossed aside, the satisfactions promised by ownership become ever more fleeting and unsatisfactory.

The "Christmas morning" excitement of new ownership and its promise of new connections and meaning have been replaced by an exhaustion of ownership and a deep-seated dissatisfaction, as the entire project of establishing relationships, purpose and meaning in a fragmenting world via consumption and ownership has essentially failed.

People sense that in seeking connection, purpose and meaning via passive consumption, they have settled for an increasingly frenzied cycle of schizophrenic distraction/ diversion.

The schizophrenia arises from the innate contradiction of the mass-production/mass media broadcast model: that you can establish your own uniqueness via ownership of an utterly non-unique, utterly ubiquitous manufactured item/consumable, and the conceit that a "one ad/brand/slogan/ideology fits all" can create the sought-after belonging, meaning and purpose via passive purchase/ ownership.

So desperate are humans for meaningful connection, identity and community that the irrationality of this model has been buried, just as "the good Germans" buried their doubts beneath the Nazi glorification of revenge, victimhood and purpose. But in sacrificing independent thought and authentic experience, the citizen has accepted a diminishment from person to consumer, from an active experience to a passive ownership and meek membership in disembodied mass-marketed simulations of belonging.

The contradiction between the desire for a unique identity and meaningful community and the purchase of store-bought identity and community via ownership of mass-produced items and mass-marketed slogans creates an alienation which cannot be bridged with more of the same or new variations on the mass-market/broadcast model.

Though marketers have seized on social networks like Facebook and MySpace with the desperation of a pack of starving canines, these models are also mere simulacrum of community. Anyone with teenagers can see the distraction/ diversion model in action: Neopets is soon replaced with Gaia which is replaced with MySpace which is replaced by Facebook, and by the time the child enters college, they have exhausted the entire universe of simulated communities. Social networks do not trumpet their inactive accounts, as they number in the tens of millions. (See below for the Polemic on Social Networking.)

The simulacrum of authenticity via the artifice of "sharing" and cleverly marketed pseudo-sincerity is akin to living on a thin gruel; the more gruel you drink, the greater your hunger for true sustenance. The desire to broadcast your "uniqueness" via lists of favorite music videos and CDs (themselves mass-produced consumables) soon runs aground on the hidden shoals of alienating contradictions described above; the "experience" of ersatz community is initially exciting/distracting, but the shallow superficiality of this "identity" and the one-line drivel that passes for "communication" and connection only widen the secret gulf within each hungry "consumer."

The quasi-religion of "branding" and "staying on message" has served to further parch an already-drought-plagued inner landscape, as the artificial communities of peer-to-peer and social networks are pressurized with the usual Standard Marketing Model overload of slogans and "mythic" imagery in service of supposedly all-important "branding."

"Building the brand" via transparent propaganda has limitations, as does the coldly robotic repetition of "staying on message;" the thin artifice of sincerity having been worn away by the mindlessness of the message, the propagandists are left with a dwindling number of tools to evince the hoped-for "mindshare/branding."

Recognition (recall the swastika) does not imply membership or belief.

Rather than engender the yearned-for connection, community and purpose, "staying on message" achieves the opposite, as the viscerally phony attempt at mind-control via robotic repetition feeds distrust and disgust.

The problem with repetition in a fragmenting world of proliferating channels is that every other brand, ideology and marketer is also busy repeating themselves, plastering their logos and catchy slogans like meth-fueled taggers frantically trying to spray every overpass and trashcan with their identity before the next tagger covers them over with his/her own "brand."

The yearning for uniqueness in a world of manufactured abundance and incessant branding manifests itself as a yearning for the experience of status and prestige—two imminently marketable and malleable traits which trace back to the competition within chimpanzee troops for reproduction rights and resources.

The endless replication of new "status symbols" has reached an apogee of absurdity, as private jets are superceded by gigantic yachts and $100 million palaces; in a world of asset bubbles, there seems to be no end of other consumers wealthy enough to top the last excess.

Due to its deep roots in the mammalian brain, this model can never be completely exhausted; but as the cycle of euphoric excess turns to one of austerity, then what constitutes prestige will change as well, as luxury consumer items and services are replaced by active, more authentic experiences.

This trend has already exploded into spas, secluded resorts and "top this" excursions to Antarctica, etc., but the market for such exclusive experiences is necessarily limited and necessarily political; when scarcity and want reign, calling attention to one's extreme wealth will not just be in poor taste, it will be dangerous.

Despite their great cost, the passivity of these services eventually creates the same dissatisfaction/ennui as any other passively consumed item or service. You can only go to the spa so many times before it too becomes boring and unfulfilling. Distraction is not a substitute for goals, meaning and purpose.

There is a certain irony to the entire marketing/propaganda machine exhausting itself just as Developed World citizens have an ever-lengthier surplus of time on their hands, just as there is an irony in the sterility of propaganda-based branding being revealed just as debt-based prosperity is replaced by credit-contraction/debt repudiation austerity.

There is additional irony in the abject failure of the Standard Model's attempts to "personalize the message" via contextual advertising and "personalized" demographics/ outreach via the simplistic methodology of data-mining past purchases. The faux online "communities" which marketers hope to exploit are akin to a Hollywood backset Western town; once they've stormed past the propped-up facade, the marketers find they've only conquered a make-believe town.

Exhibit One is this exchange in *San Francisco Chronicle* tech columnist David Einstein's May 21, 2007 Q&A:

READER: I have had Gmail for half a year, and I like it, but I am now a bit suspicious. I recently exchanged some messages with a friend from our Air Force days of 40 years ago, and I noticed that the list of "sponsored links" at the side all made reference to Air Force-related sites. Does Gmail scan message content to tailor that kind of advertising? If so, can I disable it?

A: You've had Gmail for half a year and you're just now noticing the ads alongside open messages? Guess they aren't working very well.

This summarizes the complete and abject failure of the Standard Model marketing paradigm quite concisely. The vaunted contextual ads are completely, utterly, automatically ignored. The Emperor is indeed stark naked.

Lastly, the First principle of New Media is authenticity. Since the Standard Model has long labored to co-opt or simulate authenticity via various tricks, the youthful inhabitants of New Media recognize the tricks immediately for what they are: the very acme of inauthenticity.

Polemic 2: The Social Network Facade

A visual depiction of the much-vaunted social networking phenomenon would be a phony Western town facade: a transparent attempt to simulate a real community.

If you have teenagers, or are close to teenagers, you've seen the progression: as young teens, they're enamoured with Neopets—at first with the cartoonish pets, the "locales," the games and buying and bidding (such good training for adult consumption!) and then later with the "social networking" aspects.

Once they've burned out on Neopets and their poor neopets are starving (luckily, neopets are not able to simply die from inattention from their distracted owners), then they move on to Gaia or an equivalent teen social networking site.

Here they learn that social networking is mostly about interacting with existing friends on a new forum; so in addition to email, IM'ing and talking on the phone, they can post goofy messages and so on to their friends at school.

By about 12 or 13 they're ready to enter the "bigtime" of Myspace and/or Facebook, and they quickly upload the usual panoply of "identity tags"—weird photos of themselves, their friends (again, virtually all are existing acquaintances except for the ubiquitous "Tom"), lists of favorite songs, etc.—a continuation of the model of "identity defined by what I passively consume," as lists of mass-media corporate consumables (bands, music, etc.) define an individual or provide "tags" of their personality.

The "joy" on these later-teen sites, of course, revolves around a few "activities":

1. mindless one-line messages with current friends, "communication" which could just as easily been posted as an IM or email

2. competing with siblings/pals on who has the most ersatz "friends"

3. being "edgy" via posting racy photos, listing obscure bands, etc. and making personal page as cluttered and unreadable as possible

4. Playing private detective and searching for acquaintance's home pages or pursuing some other slightly illicit-feeling voyeurism, such as visiting the pages of deceased teenagers.

Adults who venture onto these networks make feeble stabs at either copying the teenagers (more lists of favorite bands, arrghh! Why no "lists of my favorite phenomenological philosophers"?) or joining one of the thousands of forums populated with zombies (people who joined and never showed up since) or a handful of folks who try to keep some thread or topic alive.

The conversation on these forums is very similar if not identical to blog comment threads—people you don't know and don't care about posting comments that have little value other than the simulacrum of "dialog." All these simulations of communication and bonding are heavily scripted, and like cliched movie dialog the audience quickly tires of the simulation of meaning and emotion. Perhaps some people have met their future mates or good buddies on these forums but I suspect the numbers are infinitesimal compared to the tens of millions of registered users.

Once the teens tire of the project of adding flashing

bits and edgy slogans, etc. to their personal pages, and the "communication" with "friends" becomes tiresome (you might as well tell them in person tomorrow at school or IM them) then they drop out of these social networks as well, usually before they even start college.

The ersatz "Western town" has only so many attractions, and within a relatively short time the social networkers have dropped out or moved on to World of Warcraft or Second Life, similar iterations of the Potemkin Online Syndrome (POS) which engages them for some period of time (weeks, months or perhaps a few years at best) and then the whole project of simulated community and connection wears thin once again, for the dissatisfactory reality of simulacrums is all that remains after the distractions fray and the ennui and boredom set in.

Meanwhile, the marketers who spotted the fake town from afar were salivating at the rich prospects for bending young impressionable minds into consuming their products gleefully poured into the "community." Imagine their dismay when they discovered that they have conquered an empty facade town, devoid of actual community and populated by either the ghosts of former "inhabitants" (their accounts still alive but the owner long gone) or zombies on their way to the next empty facade-town and next online simulacrum of the community all humans seek.

Community cannot be manufactured with intrinsically superficial 140-character snippets of attention-deficit-disorder text and links to mass-media songs and videos. Personality cannot be expressed in scripted exchanges, nor can bonding be sustained by superficial "sharing" of cliches and mass-media fodder.

Looking Outside: An Interlude

Despite sharply higher energy and food prices, falling household wealth, rising unemployment and a host of other economic ills, the world outside our windows still seems to be proceeding along the "prosperity" vector which we have all come to believe is not just normal, but our birthright.

But beneath the apparent normalcy of the streets outside, we see disturbing evidence of the long-term transitions described above: empty storefronts, fewer shoppers, more people looking for work, falling profits, and a new cultural zeitgeist of fear and anxiety about the future.

In a very practical sense, we do not need to subscribe to expensive investment analysis reports to make projections: we need only look out the window without prejudgment. The reason is that consumers as a group are "smarter," or at least more accurate predictive indicators, than analysts, who as a group regularly fail to predict recessions and other major transitions in the economy and society.

Those of you who are incensed by the apparently unrelenting negativity of this report would do well to look outside for some period of time before proceeding. The evidence of a global phase transition is already visible in virtually every neighborhood in the U.S.

We would be well served by a skepticism for statistics, which are so easily skewed or manipulated to match pre-selected points of view.

Section Three

The Power Yet to Come

Let's begin with the principle that competitive advantage begins with insight. The key insight is that the convergence of four long-term cycles has formed a global bottleneck which will tighten for the next two decades, and every business or organization which fails to grasp the magnitude and nature of the challenges ahead will experience creative destruction.

Next, let's return to the systems-analysis principle of leverage points:

Within any complex system, there are leverage points of varying strength.

The key leverage points that are easiest to change are:
1. Add an information feedback loop
2. Change a goal
3. The most powerful leverage point, and the one most culturally and institutionally resistant to change, is a paradigm or worldview (*Weltanschauung*).

Let's start with #2, changing a goal.
The old goal was to maximize profit/stakeholder security, either bluntly stated or masked by one of the many available cliches such as "serve the customer" or "product excellence."

The new goal should be survival—to pass through the bottleneck that will destroy all but the most adaptive, flexible, insightful institutions and organizations.

To survive, each organization will need to create and sustain new bonds with its remaining customers and employees. Without these core communities, no organization will worm through the bottleneck.

If we truly understand the challenges ahead, then we will look at our customers, stakeholders and products/services in the light of FEW shortages and increasing income disparities.

In essence, a firm (or a specific division of a larger organization) can either provide some key leverage in the food, energy or water complexes which enable producers and consumers to conserve/stretch/increase-without-additional-material-inputs whatever supply of FEW assets they possess, or it can target the top 4% of the populace which will reap an ever-increasing share of remaining financial assets (income, capital, ability to borrow/leverage capital).

The Pareto Principle suggests that 4% of the populace will control most of the assets and discretionary income, 16% will still have some modest (and declining) income/assets, 48% will be struggling and 32% will make do without any meaningful discretionary income.

Even if we are vehemently opposed to and sincerely appalled by this income disparity, long-cycle price-inflation/wage-deflation waves always end with supply shortages, widespread turmoil/disruption/conflict and rising income disparities. As a business or NGO or even government agency, we have to accept these contexts and work within them. Or we can proceed with current paradigms and goals and founder.

There is no shame in closing a business or organization, and in some cases that might be the wisest course of action.

But those who wish to survive will have to transform their product line and/or services to these realities: either a product/ service greatly improves the production or conservation of life's FEW essentials for the struggling many, or it caters to the wealthy few: providing luxury, security, etc. behind discreet, politically-sensitive screens.

Recall that these cycles are not trends which can be repulsed or diverted by modest external inputs or modifying parameters; they are entelechies which are powered by internal dynamics that proceed toward predictable end-states. They are not statistical constructs or analytic artifacts; the inner logic driving each cycle is clearly visible in human history.

The Pareto Principle suggests that about 20% of every organization's employees produce 80% of the output, and only 20% of its processes/"work" produce 80% of the functional, economically viable output. To survive the bottleneck, the wise manager—even the sole proprietor—will attempt to identify the 20% of effort which is yielding 80% of the productive output and make plans to eliminate or atrophy the less-productive 80%.

As painful as it will be, managers will also have to consider identifying the 20% or so of truly productive employees and paring away the 80% less productive. Alternatively, managers might re-assign the 80% of employees producing little of value to sustainable positions that create new value. As commuting and travel become ever more costly, it may well be that 80% of the current office or warehouse space is also superfluous/ unproductive.

In an era upended by mutually reinforcing, increasingly disruptive forces, "enhancing shareholder value" and similar cliches will sound positively quaint. The paradigm will shift from boosting profit margins and negotiating richer benefit packages to survival as measured by very simple metrics: paying customers, financial solvency and some form of employee compensation.

Security will be contingent, and insecurity the norm. Those who accept and understand this worldview will suffer less and accomplish more than those who cling to the past and the petty resentments such nostalgia generates.

The most powerful leverage point, and the one most resistant to change, is a paradigm or worldview.

It is remarkably difficult for people who have lived most of their lives (i.e. the last 25 years) in a cycle of extreme credit expansion ("easy money") to adapt to the reverse condition of credit contraction ("tight money") in which there is less money, less credit, less tax revenue, less consumption, and so on. The current era of price inflation has already lasted 100 years, longer than all but the most extreme human lifespans. It is entirely natural that we are resistant to an understanding that it is about to transition to another wave, but only after a long and painful period of crisis and transformation.

From the long view, such periods of transition have occurred with astonishing regularity, as measured by prices and wages. Long phases of price stability and rising wages in the 13th, 16th and 19th centuries gave way to extended periods of sharply rising prices, stagnating wages and widespread crop failures and social disruption/conflict.

We in America are conditioned to expect more of everything, and our culture's boundless optimism seems to flow from the notion that there are no limits, either on individuals or on Nature or on our society. The realization that there will be less of everything except opportunity and the simpler happinesses will be particularly difficult for a culture which had worshipped so hopefully and longingly at the altars of mass-produced prestige and the limelight of publicity, however fleeting.

Interestingly, just as the 60s generation rebelled against the conformity, uniformity, repression and consumerism which permeated American society, the current young generation (the so-called Millennials) is already rejecting the artifice and inauthenticity of the Standard Model of marketing, even as they exhaust themselves chasing the tail of the current conformity of "identity is a list of mass-marketed items and entertainments."

It may well be that their eventual rebellion will manifest itself as a focus on trust, teamwork, optimism, and action, the very traits most needed as the old worldview of limitless resources and credit disintegrate in an extended, turbulent transformation to scarcity and conflict.

Attuned as they are to the fundamental inauthenticity of the Standard Model of marketing, they are more likely to grasp its exhaustion and embrace a new model. Those who have spent their lives in service of the Standard Model will understandably resist its demise and argue most vociferously that it will still be effective in the era ahead.

We can thus discern a brewing generational conflict in which the older managers and creators who cling to the embers of the Standard Model will be pushed aside as the limits and failures of that paradigm become ever more painfully clear.

Given that marketing is in essence communication with one's customers, the failure to communicate effectively will doom an organization regardless of the value of its product or service or the dedication of its employees or the wisdom of its managers; clinging to the Propaganda model will maroon it on the discard-side of the bottleneck.

Adding an information feedback loop

Before we discuss the leverage of adding an information feedback loop, let's review the core traits of the Standard Model of Marketing (SMOM), only one of which is a lack of robust feedback loops.

1. SMOM is inherently passive. Faced with an ad, the consumer can only act or interact in extremely proscribed ways: clip a coupon, click an web ad. This remains true even if the ad is served on YouTube or a social network, and even if it is configured by a "contextual" algorithm.

This is a reflection of the limits of social networks, which are essentially tightly scripted interactions based on materials which were once protected by copyright and are now free to anyone online. "Membership" in a passive community is limited to owning a brand of consumable—again, an essentially passive "belonging" and identity.

2. SMOM is reductive. The Standard Model's goal is to reach each individual not via an authentic individual communication with an actual unique customer but to reach some common element within millions of unique customers via a mass-media broadcast. (Adding the twist of serving an automated ad contextually is still reductionist; the software reduces individuals to various groups as measured by preconfigured metrics/contexts.)

This was always the promise of reductionism—that millions of patients could be cured by the same medication, millions of observations explained by a handful of mathematical laws, millions of voters persuaded by the same slogan and millions of consumers tapped with a single "universal" image/fantasy/message.

3. SMOM is scaled to a mass media/broadcasting

model. The Standard Model looks at individual communication as impossible, uncontrolled and costly; the apparatus is scaled to broadcasting automated ads or the same ad on mass media outlets.

4. SMOM's Prime Directive is to "stay on-message," to never stray from the Party Line. All communications are tightly scripted and controlled, which lends all SMOM the air of calculated fabrication/propaganda.

5. SMOM is Intrusive, not chosen. Ads litter every surface, every page and every screen; the consumer can select to avoid them only with special devices like TiVo or special ad-filtering software.

6. SMOM provides little to no leverage for its high cost. Installing 1,000 new billboards costs a lot, yet that addition to ad space is modest indeed. In a similar fashion, running hundreds of broadcast ads in a 24/7 clutter of thousands of ads and marketing also provides little leverage.

Part of this lack of leverage is merely statistical—any ad campaign is quickly lost amidst the shuffle—and part of it the inherent lack of information in SMOM ads and marketing. With little information, the only leverage is emotional—an essentially myth-based attempt to leverage a cultural Zeitgeist "buzz."

The proof that such leverage is deeply unpredictable is that if it were predictable, then marketers would be following the script and creating culture-moving buzz with every campaign.

7. SMOM is impatient. The metrics to measure a campaign's success are impatiently statistical: click-through rates, coupons returned, sales receipts and so on, all logged within hours or days of the ad run/blitz.

8. SMOM is statistic-based and therefore limited

to probability assessments rather than understanding internal logic. Basing an ad on previous purchases offers up rich potential for consumer mirth at the algorithm's misguided extension of past behavior, but little else. A probability does not capture the internal logic of the cycle or of an individual consumer.

Even the reliance on focus groups is fundamentally statistical, as the goal is to find representative consumers.

The inherent flaw of focus groups is the circularity of the process. The average consumer knows only what is already on the market, and as a result he/she will choose an existing product/service/model as the ideal.

Even the parsing of consumers into categories which claims an inner logic—Early Adopters, etc.—is reductive and misleading. The inner logic of an era, a group or an individual cannot be pinned down by probability, and thus the power of entelechies (i.e. the inner logic which drives and illuminates behaviors and states of mind) lies beyond the SMOM.

9. SMOM can only simulate communication. The "Dear Charles" letter, the simulacrum of actual acquaintance, the automated telemarketing call—all are patently bogus, and are reviled as such.

10. SMOM is recognized as fundamentally untrustworthy, and lacking in sincerity. In an attempt to make an end run around this universal distrust, SMOM has embraced "cloaked" marketing campaigns (shall we confess they are deceptive from inception?) in which marketing is disguised as content or "consumer messages" on weblogs and other New Media.

11. Illusory "membership" in a brand exploits the primal human longing to belong to a meaningful, powerful group.

But "belonging" via ownership of a mass-produced product is illusory, and thus unsatisfactory once the purchase "high" wears off. The essence of "branding" is to project a "group" which beckons consumers to join. Once they buy the product— their "membership" token—then the consumer experiences a dispiritingly brief and unsatisfying simulation of membership which at some level they understand is inauthentic and lifeless.

12. **SMOM is utterly predictable.** The loss-leader item will be out of stock (bait and switch); the discount requires an arduous rebate process designed to eliminate most of the discount; the ad will reach for humor; the slogan will be catchy/clever, and so on. Curiosity is sparked and satisfied in a few seconds, never to return.

13. **SMOM supports a hypocritical hierarchy.** In a 180-degree reversal of the marketing seduction, the consumer who rashly becomes a customer finds himself at the very abject bottom of the corporate pecking order. Despite the inevitable hype about "the customer is number one," Customer Service is abysmal and deceptive, frustratingly circular and seemingly designed to thwart any inquiry/demand for satisfaction.

Another way of saying this is: SMOM is disconnected from the company's true product, service and structure, and this alienation insures that the marketing will be visibly deceptive and/or inauthentic.

14. **SMOM is directional, and one-dimensional.** The goal is not to share information or educate the consumer, it is to make the sale/click/propagandize the brand/deceive the viewer. This unreflective goal captures the essential alienation and insincerity of the entire SMOM edifice.

15. **The feedback loops from consumers to marketers are sporadic and sparse to the point of being "noise."** Statistics can be gathered, data can be mined, questionnaires

can be pitched, and focus groups convened, but the flow of information and communication from these channels is so narrow and sporadic that the results are inherently suspect—the equivalent of "background noise" rather than "good data." The smaller the sample, the greater the likelihood that something important has been missed/glossed over/under-represented.

If you don't know what you don't know, then how can you discern what you're missing?

Put another way: narrow channels of feedback breed a variety of fatal errors: overestimating the value of the data, selection bias, and false causality.

Ersatz, artificial, unsustainable "communities" do not provide actual feedback loops; they provide the simulation of feedback just as they merely simulate true community.

16. SMOM purposefully nurtures a sense of "missing out" by glorifying ideals which are profoundly unrealistic. The aims are pernicious: a state of confusion/distraction punctured by sharp spikes of indulgence and deprivation.

As a corollary, SMOM works to degrade the consumer's sense of priorities, and to compress time from the "meaningful long" to the "desperate short." By setting up wildly unrealistic ideals, below which yawns a dark pit of worthlessness, the SMOM breeds a zeitgeist of insecurity, doubt, anxiety and deprivation—the perfect setup for the soul-balm of a sale.

But the cost—the utter banality and inauthenticity of the entire system of mass media /SMOM—is high, both to its practitioners/"magicians" and to its audience/victims.

Weblogs and (truly New) Media can open new, low-cost and potentially powerful information feedback loops. That is "The Power Yet to Come."

Of course their power can easily be blunted by wielding them only as platforms for the old paradigm's gimmicks and tricks—the soulless branding, the fake content passed off as authentic/useful, and so on. So it is the *potential* we discuss here, the potential to express the following characteristics.

Anyone who reads the standard finance/business media has already encountered the New Media idea of making customers your collaborators and engaging them in designing new products and services. Some global companies have already successfully implemented this idea to some degree.

What they have done is add a feedback loop that did not exist before. But there is more to it than just putting up a blog and asking for feedback; any successful weblog/New Media strategy shares these characteristics to some degree. If the mapping if cursory/minimal, then the initial enthusiasm will founder, for it is not sustainable without a deep expression of a new paradigm of marketing and communication.

Many of these ideas have found some expression in the inchoate "anti-preneur" movement; again, without a full understanding of the new paradigm, these may not be sustainable or sustain a business/organization.

These characteristics are entelechies, not trends; they are implicit in human nature and as a result cannot lose their transformative powers. All that can change is how they are described or defined.

1. Weblogs and New Media (WANM) are inherently active/interactive. Unlike a static broadcast ad or woefully narrow, tightly scripted Potemkin Village "New Media" site, there is an actual human personality to respond to as an individual, and other individuals to join/create engagement/ interaction/collaboration.

True communication and membership requires a three-way dynamic structure that can be conceptualized as a triangle. This structure elicits true communication: disagreement, personality, activity, and the excitement of being part of something great, something informative, something meaningful, something expansive which is not bound by the end-state of buying a product or service.

The New Media site offers an organization the opportunity to grow a real community which can be sustained. It is not a fad for teenagers but a source of sharing, information and engagement.

A properly designed weblog community offers layers of engagement. While the weblog moderator/host may only engage 50 members in dialog, there may be 500 other members who are content to follow the dialog as readers. Despite their lack of visible dialog, they are nonetheless self-selected members of the community who are bonded to the information, personalities and unique benefits of the site. Weblogs are thus individualistic and personal even as they are broadcast venues to the World Wide Web.

This is the key concept from which all else flows: the Standard Model paradigm is passive, the new paradigm is active. WANM invites participation, belonging, and personal connections.
The purpose of the old paradigm was persuasion via a relentlessly reductionist message; the new model's purpose is creating an authentic three-way communication/ bond/ membership/ community with authentic rewards for all parties.

The deception at the heart of the Standard Model is that "marketing" can be presented as content and nobody will be the wiser. Alas, decades of ceaseless manipulation, spin and propaganda have attuned the audience to the difference.

Just as newly developed tools of science that enable researchers to focus on the particulars of individuals—their genetic "fingerprint" and susceptibility to various illnesses—have superceded reductionist "one cure fits all" models, so weblogs enable companies and organizations to communicate with individuals/members in ways which have yet to be realized on the most profound levels.

That's the "Power Yet to Come."

The meta-message of marketing/branding is the potential for continuous betterment.

I borrow this phrase and idea from my longtime friend and fellow entrepreneur Gary F. Baker.

We each want to improve our lives, health, families, etc., and as a result we are drawn to the promise of doing so. This is the essence of consumerism: here is a product, service or brand that will provide consistent betterment.

As discretionary spending shrinks, consumers will still crave the hope and optimism of continuous betterment even as their ability to purchase goods and services declines.

The new paradigm of active participation in an authentic community offers the ideal paradigm for engaging the consumer/visitor in the process of designing/ providing continuous betterment, and in so doing, creating that betterment in their lives.

The profound power of Open Source software is that 10,000 programmers collaborating of their own free will can improve and adapt a product much better, faster and cheaper than 100 paid programmers working for one enterprise. Their engagement doesn't just better the product—it also enriches their lives with commitment, optimism, community and the sense of belonging to something exciting which is larger than their own involvement and life.

This is in essence the model of the "Power Yet to Come:" freely chosen engagement that offers continual betterment of the community, members and product/service.

Can this be profitable?

Perhaps the best answer is another question: in an era of crisis and turmoil, is there any other way to be profitable? I believe the answer is already abundantly clear: no.

Perhaps their engagement brings in no immediate revenue. But if an organization's weblog and New Media sites offer a consumer/visitor value, community and the opportunity for continuous betterment, then the products and services which result from this collaboration will have a broad audience/appeal/ market, as they were designed and adapted by a large base of potential customers.

The adaptive power of an engaged, authentic community is analogous to the stupendous powers of natural selection; as the product/service/community grows and evolves, more adaptations or possibilities present themselves. The richer the pool of possibilities, the more robust and adaptable the organism. In this case, the organism is the organization or enterprise. Those with weak "genes" and poor adaptive abilities will not make it through the bottleneck; they will end up on the discard pile of history.

2. WANM is individualistic and responsive. Rather than attempt to attract customers or stakeholders with reductionist messages or images, WANM does the hard, rewarding work of communicating directly with individual members/customers.

To the degree they invite participation, sharing of

experience and spontaneity, weblogs enable belonging and connection.

Who do you think will be the more likely and loyal customer—one bombarded with endless streams of propaganda and advertising on which you've spent millions, or one who has chosen to join your weblog community and who your weblog host invites to a special tour of your plant/floor? Which one has a higher degree of connecting with a user/customer? Which one is more cost-effective? In the long run, which costs less?

3. WANM enables both individual and broadcast communication. An ad or static New Media site offers nothing more meaningful to the individual than an opportunity to buy a product or type a few words which he/she knows are meaningless to the degree that they will go unnoticed by those in charge of the site.

A weblog that embodies and expresses WANM characteristics offers much more: a dialog with a company personality, a real person, other users and other employees.

In that anyone on the Web can stop by and read these exchanges as a visitor (non-member), then the blog also scales to broadcast the organization's purpose, products, services and commitments.

The dialog (personal, occasionally messy and therefore lively) is broadcasted to others. The meta-message is abundantly clear: here you find honesty, personality, collaboration, value, and community.

4. WANM's Prime Directive is to clear a space for trust, honest dialog and meaningful contribution. The key tenet of propaganda is to "stay on-message" in order to plant via pure repetition suspect truths in a numbed, distracted, audience anxious for meaning and connections to something worthy of their loyalty and trust.

The concept of a "clearing" is deceptively profound. The old paradigm was based on the hidden belief that uncontrolled communication would loose the banshees of destruction upon the organization, that a single word or phrase could be misconstrued and pivot the public/consumer perception from neutral or positive to wildly negative.

Ironically, the only way to do this is to prevaricate, obscure, misdirect or cloak—all the techniques of dishonesty and propaganda that we have all learned to recognize and loathe.

Yet despite the healing power of honesty and forthrightness, corporations, agencies and organizations still cling to the model which invites destruction of trust, communication, sympathy and connection: maintaining a tightly controlled, unresponsive, unyielding script which lays out a narrative of blamelessness, corporate caring, and so on—all of which is nullified by the meta-message of anxious over-control: the only reason to do this is if you have something to hide.

The opposite of "staying on-message" is a clearing which has been consciously opened for real, unscripted communication and contributions in which an individual's words and offerings are presented as worthy and meaningful in the context of a community worthy of belonging/membership.

Put another way: The ecology of marketing is threatened by any clearing in which honest dialog, skepticism and participation can grow. The ecology of marketing depends on a thicket of monocultural messages: identical, repetitive, and pernicious.

Honesty requires both risk and vulnerability. The supposedly lowest-risk strategy is to "stay on-message" and divulge nothing that might be so honest as to spark dismay, disapproval or controversy. Yet this strategy also negates authenticity and trust, guaranteeing the message will be rejected as misleading, manipulative, patently deceptive, etc. The meta-message is: we don't trust you.

Humans build connections—that is, sympathy, empathy, understanding—by sharing our vulnerabilities and frailties. This will not change. The "Power Yet to Come" paradigm doesn't back away in fear from honesty and vulnerability—it actively embraces both the risk and the vulnerability, for these are the keys to the kingdom of trust and authenticity.

5. WANM is chosen by the user. Potential customers may be invited via email or an ad, but their visit is voluntary. For them to visit again, useful information and an opportunity to contribute in a triangular dynamic (me, a shared focus and you) must be present.

We ignore ads but are avid about sites which engage us.

6. WANM provides enduring leverage at low cost. Customer loyalty is supposedly a cherished goal, but experience of marketing and customer service speaks of a profound disconnect between the public relations/propaganda and the actual resources invested in customers.

Here is an anecdote that expresses the old paradigm's core failures to perfection. My father has long been a loyal customer of Ford vehicles, and specifically the Lincoln Continental nameplate. The transmission on his current Lincoln developed a serious problem that required replacement. Alas, the vehicle, though by no means old, was no longer under the company's limited warranty. Ford refused to replace the transmission at its own expense. My father paid the bill, but after some 30+ years as a loyal customer, his next automobile was a Chrysler.

Did Ford possess any sight that recognized customer loyalty as the essential ingredient of their future sales/success? Apparently not. How much did Ford Motor Company spend on mostly ignored/worthless "branding" and advertising? Tens of millions. What if they'd spent $30 million replacing defective, worn-before-their-time transmissions in their most expensive vehicles for their most loyal customers? Which strategy would garner the more enduring loyalty and sales? Which "meta-message" is more meaningful and enduring? Hint: it's not the ads.

To offer useful information, the opportunity to contribute to a worthy endeavor or group, to be part of a larger, meaningful community, to be offered value rather than hype—these impact an individual customer more than an entire lifetime of advertisements and marketing shamelessly (and futilely) disguised as "content."

7. WANM is patient and aimed for enduring loyalty and engagement. The new paradigm is based on the insight that few will pass through the bottlenecks ahead—few customers and few enterprises. Therefore the organization which wants to survive must identify with its stakeholders in fundamentally new ways. Customer and employee loyalty cannot be bought cheaply, or with tricks; it must be earned over months, years and even decades.

From this point of view, click-through rates and "impressions" lose their value as metrics of anything remotely relevant to the organization's survival in an era of turmoil and disruption.

8. WANM enables the internal logic of a member/potential customer/group to reveal itself. No statistical/heuristic/algorithmic model can ever identify or reduce the inner states of humans; the belief that probabilities offer a substitute for understanding inner states/inner logic/entelechies is essentially religious, for there is no evidence to support the belief.

9. WANM clears space for true communication. Old Media, fake-New Media and SMOM are *a priori* one-way—the "message" is transmitted from the marketing "magician" or mass media to the user or consumer, who is allowed to "interact" in meaningless, scripted simulations of "conversation" and in "sharing" snippets of other mass media products (videos, pre-packaged opinions, one-line comments, etc.)

True communication is actually three-way: it requires an opening/clearing, an object or topic of focus, and open communication between a moderator and one or more members.

In the SMOM, the "focus" is convincing the consumer to buy the product/service or form a propagandized positive impression of the brand; that topic is exhausted in a matter of seconds, and hence the irretrievability of authenticity in mass-media/SMOM settings masquerading as New Media.

10. WANM earns the user/member's trust and sincerity. Trust is earned, not bestowed. The New paradigm focuses the energy and budget of an enterprise or organization not on artifice and deception but on forging bonds with customers by offering them trustworthy information, service and the opportunity to contribute to a greater, worthy community of other customers/visitors.

11. The primal human longing to belong to a meaningful, influential group is the heart of the new paradigm. The structure of weblogs and New Media sites maps the purpose: to provide value and membership based not on a superficial brand but on the opportunity to contribute and collaborate on a worthy focus: providing useful information, improving a product or service, or expanding it beyond its original bounds.

Trust, teamwork, optimism, and action: these are the bywords of the new paradigm, not for employees but for employees and customers/members/visitors.

12. WANM thrives on surprise and curiosity. In successful blogs, personality replaces sterile branding and mind-numbing "on message" repetition. This is the fundamental reason why individual's blogs gather millions of users on a marketing/ad budget of zero dollars while corporate blogs remain in a decidedly non-influential zone.

Control of every message is the antithesis of personality. Thus the organization has to select the right kind of moderator— positive and real, able to engage honestly as opposed to "canned" scripts which might as well be automated for all the warmth and character they express.

Curiosity leads to interaction that fosters surprise. A real personality always retains the potential for surprise while ads and marketing do not. The right person as moderator/host will spark curiosity in employees, visitors and customers alike because curiosity and enthusiasm in meeting people and being useful are infectious.

Data and wikis are faceless and thus limited. Neither enables personal communication or broadcasting to a wider audience.

13. In WANM, marketing and customer services are one. In essence, any enterprise's blog or New Media site is customer service. Any inquiry posted to the blog is routed to dedicated staff, not a call center. Service staffers are assigned an account/customer for the duration of their employment at the company so the customer isn't dealing with a faceless new entity (computer or person? Who knows?) with each contact.

Customer service and the community of customers/ visitors/stakeholders is the same interface, the same site, the same paradigm. The weblogs and New Media are integrated into the company much like a new helical strand of DNA; there is no single strand or employee who isn't connected to the customer, visitor, member, stakeholder via the weblogs and New Media sites.

14. WANM is dynamic, multidimensional, adaptive; it expresses the will and concerns of its members/audience as well as those of employees and managers. Community is sharing, learning, utility, information, connection. Rather than establish yet another stale one-way vector of force-fed "message" and simulated communication ("we take your concerns very seriously, blah, blah, blah"), WANM nurtures a dynamic ecology.

The customers dream would be to join a community of users, employees and managers which actually quickly resolves their service problems regardless of the "trouble" or cost, and one which allowed them to contribute their experience, and yes, their difficulties, for the betterment of other customers and the enterprise's future response and products.

The enterprise's dream would be customers who essentially co-design a new product or service faster, better, cheaper and enable an "insanely great" product via their collaboration, enthusiasm and evangelism.

Both are entirely possible, indeed, inevitable, if the new paradigm (what I call "The Power Yet to Come") is truly understood and wound into the organization's DNA.

15. WANM is essentially expansive, flexible feedback loops that feed contributions and collaborations. Once clearings are opened, feedback loops which might not have been originally foreseen will grow, much like new neuronal connections in a healthy, stimulated brain.

Exactly which loops will grow will depend on the managers' ability to keep the clearing free of thickets of bias, procedure, inertia and the weeds of the old paradigm, on the organizations' transformation, adaptations, markets, ecology, etc., and on the enthusiasm and personalities of the organization's moderators/evangelists/bloggers.

The most important step is to create the clearing and provide the structure. Much like a bean plant and a trellis, the organism (feedback loops) will thrive if just given the sunlight and air and structure to do so.

Put another way: the structure enables triangulated learning by providing the purpose, goals and challenges for customers, employees, managers, visitors, et al. to focus on and share. People want to contribute and to be part of the solution; the new paradigm empowers them to do so.

The models of connection are not difficult to grasp; we employ them every day: being heard, mentoring, confirmation, debate, bonding, etc.

Since the new paradigm is scaled to human interaction, it can scale from "local" to "global."

16. WANM's tropism is for authenticity over artifice and unrealistic mythic projections. These are words which encapsulate the new paradigm of "The Power Yet to Come": experience, dialog, resolution, trust; engagement/interaction/collaboration; listening, disagreement, personality, activity, excitement, membership in a dynamic, meaningful, useful, positive, growing community/group.

The Standard Model of Marketing sought to snare essentially unwary consumers with subconscious traps based on mythic desires for prestige, completeness, membership in an elite, and so on.

Mythic images and words appeal directly to these deeply

subconscious drives and desires, bypassing the rational mind. This subterfuge, no matter how successful, is limited by it false nature. The status, membership and power which was promised by the ad or brand is *a priori* fleeting in nature, and the consumer is left with a perplexing and pervasive sense of dissatisfaction and ennui.

The new paradigm, on the other hand, promises another kind of limbic connection and stimulation: a real dialog, a real membership, a real dynamism—everything which the brand or ad promised but could never deliver.

Can any online community offer a substitute for living, breathing family, friends and community? Of course not. Nonetheless, those who have experienced true online community know just how deep and fond the bonds can be, despite the fact that the members do not even know what their friends look like.

My nephew, who has Type I diabetes, was once on an online forum he frequents when he slipped into a diabetic state of shock. His correspondent at the time noted his behavior and, knowing he was diabetic, realized something was deeply amiss. She called 911 and was able to nurse an address out of my fast-fading nephew. Her caring, quick thinking and intervention from Texas (my nephew was in Oregon) literally saved his life.

Now that is a dramatic example, but there are millions of other examples of real bonds and communities forming online, often centered on blogs or New Media forums.

Based on my own site's sustained, dramatic growth in readership and community, and my observations, research and conversations with other successful bloggers, I believe there are discrete growth stages characteristic of all blogs and New Media sites:

1. An initial launch plateau characterized by low traffic and few links.

2. Discovery spikes of traffic and links as people discover the value of the site.

3. Temporary growth plateaus as some "discovery" visitors exhaust their interest or connection and leave.

4. As long as the site continues adding value and feedback loops, additional discovery spikes lead to periods of renewed growth.

5. As a result, the trendline of visitors, interest, links and shared information continues to rise.

Section Four

Examples of The Power Yet to Come

Of the many possible examples, I have selected what I hope is a representative sampling. Two recent corporate campaigns that illustrate some of the above ideas (both received wide media coverage) were Starbucks' involvement of its customers in improving their offerings and service, and Dell Computer's efforts to improve their customer service. A Web search will bring up the extensive coverage should you wish to learn more about those two oft-lauded campaigns.

Are these highly visible campaigns sustainable? Only time will tell if they embody enough of the new paradigm entelechies to endure and grow.

1. Retail/Merchandising

First, let's acknowledge that the potential customer base for top-tier department store retailers will always be limited, and is poised to become even more so; but even if 25% of the workforce is unemployed, some percentage of the other 75% will still have discretionary income. And those with the handsomest salaries will typically be the ones most hard-pressed to find the time for gift selection and personal shopping. Even in times of turmoil and recession, life in the form of gift giving and other rituals of family and friendship go on. One way to approach this in the new paradigm would be to leverage what the top-tier retailer already offers for free: personal buyers.

Unbeknownst to most customers, a national chain of upscale department stores offers "personal buyer" services at no extra cost to its customers. If a customer needs help selecting gifts, or would appreciate some assistance in choosing an outfit, the personal buyer is available to help.

If I didn't know a manager in this division, I would never have known such a service existed, as it remains largely unpromoted by the retailer.

Were I engaged to boost sales of this division, I would first set up a separate New Media site for the service, and work with each buyer to post their personal weblog.

Their personalities, tastes and design sensibility would be shared with customers and visitors, along with photos of their recent design choices for clients. Any visitor to the site would soon learn which buyer he/she would like to engage. They would come to "know" the buyer through the blog and the other customers the buyer has helped. Even if they didn't engage a buyer, they would find the solutions and tips entertaining and useful in terms of their own shopping. While only 50 customers might add a comment or engage in a dialog, 500 or 5,000 potential customers might find the exchange worth reading and following. Even if they provide no sign of engagement, their own experience (repeat visits) shows that they are indeed engaged and interested.

I would also suggest that it was important to discuss mistakes and disappointments on the blogs, and that a variety of buyers should be hired so that a wide range of cultural, age and taste differences could be accommodated. The personal buyers would not necessarily be fulltime; they could have other duties, but each should enjoy being personal buyers.

I would also set up a forum for customers, buyers and other employees where questions about any merchandise or complaints could be aired and answered. Casual visitors would then learn via this meta-communication that this store took its customer service seriously, and was not afraid to candidly post the results publicly.

Customers could also post notes and gift/buying tips for other customers, and schedule appointments (online or in person) with the personal buyer of their choice.

The store would then mention the service site and personal buyer blogs in its emails and communications with its best customers and on its Web portal. When new buyers are hired/launched, then their blog will be posted and passed on to customers along with the usual announcement of sales and discounts.

Over time, customers would visit the personal buyer blogs just out of curiosity. If the personalities were varied enough and authentic enough, they would return for the information and the fun of seeing what others had picked.

Shopping is a certain kind of fun, and the personal buyer's goal is to continuously improve the customer's experience—even if they end up buying nothing. The customer who enjoyed the experience of reviewing the buyers' blogs, reading their design tips and "case studies," becoming acquainted with their personalities and quirks, will come back because their curiosity, desire for useful information and fun will be engaged.

If they want to begin a dialog with a specific personal buyer, they can post a message on his/her blog or email him/her.

Let's assume even the upscale customer's budget might tighten; which store will he/she go to for any gifts or wardrobe additions? The one with the faceless, static adverts or the one with Gigi, the personal shopper who is so engaging and fun and who answers blog posts and email queries with interesting, information-filled replies? Which would you go to? And of course Gigi and her colleagues can offer you special discounts and sales unavailable elsewhere.

Some customers will waste buyers' time; this is the nature of retail. We cannot know the internal logic running inside each customer's minds, but we can know the internal logic common to all humans seeking a fun or informative retail/shopping experience.

Such a New Media site with personality and information-rich weblogs hosted by easily-accessible personal buyers and a forum for any questions or customer service problem (backed by the staff to resolve each query quickly and completely) would enable a level of customer (and employee) engagement and loyalty which no other structure could possibly match.

Which department store will survive the compression of customer's discretionary budgets—the one investing in building and enriching a community of customers and potential customers, or the one pouring money into static print and Web advertising which are largely ignored?

2. Vehicle Manufacturer
In the future, extremely energy-efficient vehicles will be desirable products. Whether the manufacturer hopes to sell 1,000 vehicles or 10,000,000, it will be facing a staggering global glut of manufacturing capacity and formidable competition from established companies and startups alike.

Bringing the customer into the loop of design, manufacturing, knowledge and events in their locale would be one way to leverage the competitive advantages of the new paradigm.

If I were asked to suggest a new-paradigm strategy for either a global company or a startup, it would center around a weblog/New Media site which acted as a forum for all sorts of vehicle/energy information, not just the manufacturer's own products.

I would suggest hiring a host/moderator with an engaging personality and a zealous interest in vehicles, technology, energy efficiency, etc. He/she (I would recommend having both male and female moderators) would be free to express their own views with the usual disclaimer they didn't represent the company's views. The meta-message is the company isn't afraid to post consumer-guide data or discussions that are not marketing for their products. Competition exists, and the company's meta-communicating that it welcomes competition.

As with the above example, a key feature is presenting a variety of lively, informed, friendly hosts/moderators for visitors and potential customers to choose from. Eventually the "gearheads" will gather round the most gearhead-friendly moderator, while various other identities/groups will be drawn to other hosts.

If a moderator/host eventually attracts a readership/community of 5,000 people, who do you think is more likely to actually buy a vehicle: one of those well-informed, engaged members of that community who has received special offers and information, been invited to a low-key VIP test drive, someone who has contributed to the community with questions or experiences, or someone glancing at a static ad presented to millions of restless, distracted viewers on some mass-media screen?

One of the special offers to blog community members would be a special factory/floor tour. Just get to the factory, and the company would host you, give you a unique shirt commemorating your visit, enable a visit /talk with a designer or engineer, lunch with the floor employees, elicit your views on improving the vehicles, and explain the challenges/trade-offs which have been wrestled with in the design and manufacturing process.

A key part of the tour would be showing how the company manufactures vehicles for individuals—how a customer can order a car to their specifications within the parameters of the factory.

After the tour, the blog moderator would continue to communicate with the group as a group, giving the meta-message that the company wants further engagement. The "hard sell" would not exist; the entire site would be about sharing information, ideas and special offers such as "VIP test drives" for the site community's members, and updates which included the experience of members of the group who bought a vehicle from the company—even if it is a used vehicle.

As always, customer service would be integrated like two strands of DNA; existing customers with questions or problems would share the same forum.

The opportunity to build a community of interested (and thus potential customers and/or evangelists) citizenry is present; all an enterprise has to do is understand how adding that rich feedback loop will leverage their business in ways no other marketing can possibly match.

3. Pizza Shop

Even in a global recession, most consumers will be able to splurge on the occasional pizza. Whether the business is a global franchise or a single pizza purveyor, the idea is the same: engage the customers in a worthy project that offers continuous betterment.

As an example, the new site/weblog would ask customers to help "design" "the healthiest pizza." The various "designs" would be winnowed down with the moderator's collaboration—yes, cost would be a factor upfront—and then customers could, for a limited time, be able to order the various pizza pies they helped "build".

In conjunction with the "healthiest pizza" project, the store would offer real salads for sale without gobs of calorie-heavy salad dressing—a truly healthy addition to the pizza. Various recipes for salads or similar "healthy additions" would be solicited and posted on the site for the continuous betterment of customer's health.

This could easily be degraded to a gimmick, of course, but the benefits of the campaign would really only flow if the concern for improving customer's diet and health were authentic, and if customers and visitors were encouraged to contribute (via discounts, special offers, contests, etc.) their own ideas, recipes and healthy-diet tips. The key idea here is to engage the potential customer and past customer in a larger project—improving their health and the health of others, with pizza being presented as simply one part—a potentially healthier part even as it remains "fun food"—of this larger purpose.

4. Builder/Contractor

As shortages and financial disruptions roil the global marketplace, many entrepreneurs and workers will find their previous occupations and businesses have vanished, or been leapfrogged. The new paradigm offers an excellent avenue to building a new business and/or occupation.

Certainly one of the sectors hardest hit by the recession and credit contraction is new housing and commercial construction. If I were asked to help out-of-work contractors and craftspeople find a new livelihood, I would start by suggesting they set up a New Media site centered around a network of resources for improving energy efficiency and resource conservation "faster, better, cheaper."

Since some 70% of non-transportation energy in the U.S. is consumed by buildings, there are enormous opportunities for saving consumers and businesses money with retrofits and alternative energy installations.

For the contractor or tradesperson, the key is to assemble the resources needed to learn everything they can about the engineering, cost, installation and "tricks of the trade" for solar installations—hot water systems, photovoltaic, and window treatments (films which can be applied to glass, etc.)

Thus a carpenter should seek an engineer with the skills to design the strengthening required for a warehouse roof to support an array of solar panels. Some of this proactive—calling engineers, stopping by jobsites and the like. The new paradigm doesn't replace footwork and networking in person—it only provides ways to leverage what you have learned and the network of people you know.

The key idea is to seek to recruit via a New Media site like-minded people in the trades and engineering who are also dedicated to establishing a new livelihood. The next key is to recruit mentors who can guide and advise members on the best practices, both in the new energy/building field but also in providing a higher level of customer service than is typical in the industry. As always in the new paradigm, information, dialog, sharing and customer service are bound together like strands of DNA.

Once the site is rich enough in information and resources, potential customers will be drawn to the site, especially if there is an interactive forum where their questions and own experience are solicited and valued.

Who is more likely to want your firm to retrofit their home or add a solar array to their building—someone scanning the

Yellow Pages online or a static "other consumers opinion" site, or a site where their questions have been addressed and their own experience solicited?

As always, the goal should be to present a number of different faces as hosts; the U.S. is a very multicultural and diverse society, and people will be drawn to people who they feel comfortable with. For instance, a single female homeowner might feel more comfortable in a group hosted by a knowledgeable female.

Unfortunately, there may well be few "help wanted: windmill installer" ads online; the new paradigm approach would be to learn how to save potential customers money within a few months, or cut their future energy/resource bills to as near-zero as possible, and then assemble a network of people who can share this expertise and actually install it in the real world.

If the benefits are presented without hype, and customer service is built into the genes of the site/forum, then the competitive advantages of the new paradigm will boom.

I would end by noting once again that the Standard Model is impatient, the new paradigm is patient; results will accrue over time as expertise, interaction and customer service improve/grow.

5. Community Food Bank

Hunger has long been a global concern and it will increasingly challenge even nations like the U.S. A prodigious amount of edible food is wasted every day in the U.S., largely for want of a channel to distribute it to hungry citizens.

A community (non-profit) food bank organization might find that a New Media site would greatly leverage their efforts to collect food that would otherwise go to waste and direct it to the needy.

As always, the kernel concept is to create a forum that offers information and opportunities to become engaged and contribute as well as to learn. A key part of fighting hunger is improving knowledge of nutrition and food; for instance, the "best used by" dating system in the U.S. food packaging industry has evolved into a stunningly wasteful "throw out by this date" obsession, even though the dating protocol inevitably understates the actual shelf-life of the product or foodstuff.

Alleviating hunger is not just about providing food, but providing healthy food, which nowadays means overcoming the powerful propaganda promulgated by the fast-food and prepared-food industries.

Thus the food bank forum would seek to engage not just potential household donors and volunteers to collect the food but the recipients and major donor partners, such as churches and other faith-based organizations.

Potential donors could visit the site to learn where their canned goods and fresh food items could be dropped off, and where they could volunteer a few hours, even occasionally. Recipients and donors alike could share recipes and nutrition tips, and as always in the new paradigm, a variety of hosts and voices would be encouraged to maximize engagement and contribution of visitors, donors and recipients.

Such a site could incorporate church, NGO (non-governmental organization) and local government resources, enabling these groups to "spread the word" without requiring budgeting their own resources to outreach/communication.

It should be noted here that a volunteer moderator would not need to be full-time; a moderator could host a nutrition forum, for instance, in his/her spare time. Since the forum would be soliciting contributions from donor restaurants, food wholesalers and household donors, recipes, tips and other information would soon begin flowing into the site as the benefits (community, the fulfillment of contributing, the information gained, the increase in donations and so on) become known.

People want to help. Giving them an easy, rewarding way to do so is as simple as adding a multi-stranded feedback loop for them to enter.

The Power Yet to Come

Could a municipal water district's service be improved with a new-paradigm site? Could a community college, a planning commission, a law office or a non-profit gain any value from actively engaging its stakeholders? I believe the answer is yes, though the specifics would depend on the audience, stakeholders, and many other elements.

What about a large enterprise which serves only a handful of customers? In those cases, perhaps the audience that would benefit most from a new-paradigm site would be the employees and managers tasked with getting the organization through the coming bottleneck.

I cannot predict which permutation or combination of the above principles will work best for your organization or enterprise. I can only repeat that the principles are leverage points that are missing from the Standard Models of Marketing and customer service—leverage points that can offer powerful, flexible competitive advantages in the extremely challenging era ahead.

www.ingramcontent.com/pod-product-compliance
Lightning Source LLC
Chambersburg PA
CBHW060148200526
45165CB00023B/1339